They are DESCENDANTS of GREY WOLVES.

3

There are MORE than 400 DOG BREEDS.

Totally AMAZING FACTS ABOUT DOGS

raintree

a Capstone company — publishers for children

DOGS
HAVE BEEN DOMESTICATED FOR AT LEAST

15,000 YEARS.

THE UNITED STATES HAS MORE DOGS THAN ANY OTHER COUNTRY.

DOGS WERE ONCE BANNED AS PETS IN ICELAND.

I OBJECT!

THERE ARE NEARLY 90 MILLION PET DOGS IN THE USA.

 DOGS ARE KEPT AS PETS IN MANY PARTS OF THE WORLD.

But in **SOME** countries, dogs are used for **FOOD!**

WHAT?!

When livestock became **DOMESTICATED,** dogs **HERDED** and **PROTECTED** them as well.

DOGS CAN LEARN UP TO 250 WORDS.

The Daily Dog News

13

SOME DOGS ARE ABLE TO SMELL AND IDENTIFY CANCER IN HUMANS.

15

MAX IS THE MOST POPULAR NAME FOR **MALE** DOGS.

BELLA IS THE MOST POPULAR NAME FOR FEMALE DOGS.

DOGS HAVE A BASIC UNDERSTANDING OF MATHS.

BORDER COLLIES ARE ONE OF THE CLEVEREST DOG BREEDS.

Just call me EINSTEIN!

THE GERMAN SHEPHERD IS THE TOP **POLICE** AND **MILITARY** DOG BREED.

The film *Rex* is based on a **TRUE STORY** about a **US MARINE** and her **COMBAT DOG, SERGEANT REX.**

A DOG HAS 200-300 MILLION SCENT RECEPTORS IN ITS NOSE.

A DOG'S SENSE OF SMELL IS 1,000 TIMES BETTER THAN A HUMAN'S.

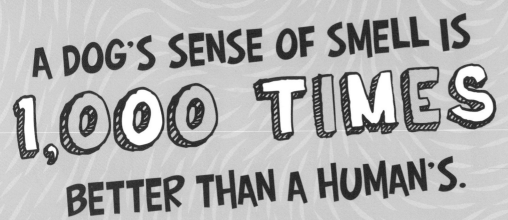

A dog's brain releases the "happy chemical", **OXYTOCIN**, when it spends time with some humans and other dogs.

Life is pretty **WONDERFUL** right now!

DOGS CAN ALSO FEEL JEALOUS!

DOGS HAVE AROUND 1,700 TASTE BUDS.

28

HUMANS HAVE ABOUT 9,000!

THE **WETNESS** OF A DOG'S NOSE IS ACTUALLY A **THIN LAYER** OF MUCUS.

THE MUCUS HELPS THE DOG TO **SMELL**.

A DOG'S NORMAL BODY TEMPERATURE IS **38.3-39.2** DEGREES CELSIUS (101-102.5 DEGREES FAHRENHEIT).

A small dog's heart BEATS between 100–140 TIMES PER MINUTE.

MORE THAN 40% OF DOGS SLEEP IN BED WITH THEIR OWNERS.

ALMOST 70% of dog owners think their DOG KNOWS when a STORM is coming.

A SPECIAL MEMBRANE IN A DOG'S EYES HELPS IT TO SEE AT NIGHT.

THE MEMBRANE IS CALLED THE TAPETUM LUCIDUM.

DO YOUR DOG'S PAWS SMELL LIKE POPCORN?

PUPPIES CAN SLEEP FOR AS MUCH AS **20 HOURS A DAY!**

Puppies are born DEAF and BLIND.

DOGS HAVE ABOUT 320 BONES!

PUPPIES have 28 TEETH.

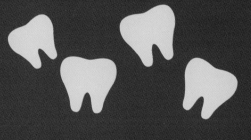

ADULT dogs have 42 TEETH.

IT IS A NATURAL INSTINCT FOR DOGS TO SPIN BEFORE LYING DOWN. DOGS NATURALLY CURL UP WHEN THEY SLEEP.

Z Z ZZZZ

This position PROTECTS vital organs and keeps dogs WARM.

STROKING A DOG CAN LOWER YOUR BLOOD PRESSURE.

MOCHI THE SAINT BERNARD HOLDS THE WORLD RECORD FOR LONGEST DOG TONGUE AT **18.58 CENTIMETRES** (7.31 INCHES) LONG.

An **AUSTRALIAN CATTLE DOG** called

BLUEY

lived to be **29 YEARS** and **5 MONTHS** old.

CONGRATULATIONS

He holds the world record for OLDEST DOG.

BASENJIS HAVE BEEN LIVING WITH HUMANS FOR A LONG TIME!

IN FACT, SOME PEOPLE SAY BASENJIS WERE GIVEN TO EGYPTIAN PHARAOHS AS GIFTS.

AW

WOOO! AWWOOO!

BASENJIS DON'T BARK – THEY YODEL!

The WORLD'S SHORTEST dog is a CHIHUAHUA called MILLY.

At just **9.7 CENTIMETRES (3.8 INCHES) TALL,** she's shorter than a **CAN OF FIZZY DRINK!**

NORWEGIAN LUNDEHUNDS HAVE

SIX TOES

ON EACH FOOT.

They can **CLOSE THEIR EARS** and **TIP THEIR HEADS**

ALL THE WAY BACK.

A GREAT PYRENEES CALLED DUKE WON THE MAYORAL ELECTION THREE TIMES RUNNING IN CORMORANT, MINNESOTA, USA.

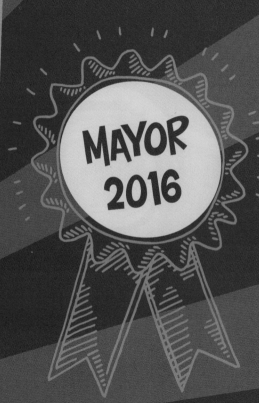

VOTE

DUKE

MAYOR 2016

NEWFOUNDLANDS

HAVE WEBBED FEET!

They are also known as "Newfies".

63

Dalmatian puppies are born all WHITE!

They develop their SPOTS later on in life.

A BORDER COLLIE CALLED CHASER IS THOUGHT TO BE THE WORLD'S CLEVEREST DOG.

SHE CAN **RECOGNIZE** THE **NAMES** OF MORE THAN **1,000** OBJECTS!

ORIENT, A GERMAN SHEPHERD GUIDE DOG, successfully led his BLIND OWNER along the APPALACHIAN TRAIL.

The trek took 8 MONTHS.

DOGS CAN BE TRAINED TO HELP PEOPLE WHO ARE HAVING SEIZURES.

They lie next to their owners to PREVENT INJURY.

Dogs have at least
18 MUSCLES
in each ear.

THEY CAN SHUT OFF THEIR INNER EAR TO DROWN OUT DISTRACTING SOUNDS.

BASSET HOUNDS

have some of the **LONGEST EARS** of any breed.

If I flap them hard enough, do you think **I COULD FLY?!**

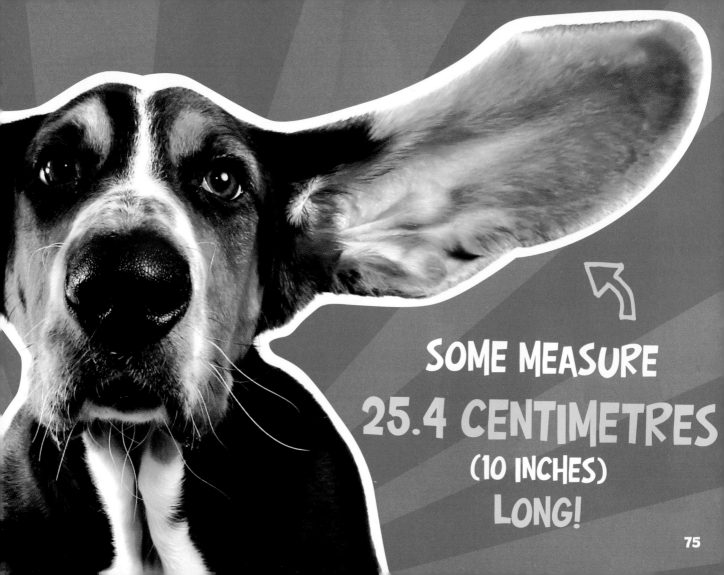

SOME MEASURE
25.4 CENTIMETRES
(10 INCHES)
LONG!

A SERVICE DOG CALLED KIRSCH RECEIVED AN HONORARY DEGREE FROM JOHNS HOPKINS UNIVERSITY.

(HE WENT TO EVERY LECTURE WITH HIS OWNER, CARLOS.)

DOGS CAN HEAR SOUNDS OF 35,000 VIBRATIONS PER SECOND.

HUMANS CAN ONLY HEAR

20,000

VIBRATIONS PER SECOND.

It's said that the BRUSSELS GRIFFON breed was the inspiration for the EWOK characters in the STAR WARS films.

POMERANIANS

WEIGH JUST 3.2-4.5 KILOGRAMS
(7-10 POUNDS).

That's about the same weight as the average watermelon.

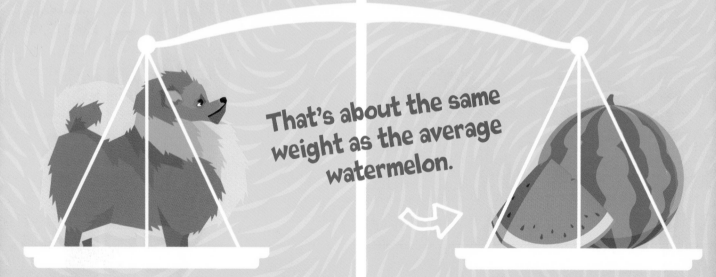

83

A CHIWEENIE
is a cross between a
CHIHUAHUA and a DACHSHUND.

ALTHOUGH SMALL, CHIWEENIES **BARK** TO PROTECT LOVED ONES. THEY CAN BE GREAT GUARD DOGS!

MANNY
THE
FRENCHIE

IS A
FAMOUS
FRENCH
BULLDOG.

He became popular on INSTAGRAM, where his owner POSTED pictures of him SNOOZING IN A SINK.

HE WAS NAMED ONE OF THE MOST INFLUENTIAL PETS IN 2017.

DOGS HAVE SOME SWEAT GLANDS IN THEIR PAWS.

But
PANTING
is their
main way of
**COOLING
DOWN.**

IT IS A MYTH THAT DOGS ONLY SEE IN **BLACK** AND **WHITE.**

DOG VISION

THEY SEE SOME COLOUR, BUT NOT AS VIVIDLY AS HUMANS.

HUMAN VISION

MOST
DOGS
HAVE
PINK
TONGUES.

BUT CHOW CHOWS AND SHAR-PEIS HAVE **BLACK** TONGUES!

GREYHOUNDS ARE THE FASTEST DOG BREED.

THEY CAN RUN UP TO

72 KILOMETRES
(45 MILES)

PER HOUR.

Some dog owners give their pets GIFTS on BIRTHDAYS and SPECIAL OCCASIONS.

SOME ALSO
INCLUDE
THEIR PUP
ON THE
**FAMILY
CHRISTMAS
CARD.**

One study says that some dogs align themselves with EARTH'S MAGNETIC FIELD while they POO.

GEORGE WASHINGTON LOVED DOGS.

He had a **FRENCH HOUND** called VULCAN and a **DALMATIAN** called MADAM MOOSE.

THE AZTECS ONCE WORSHIPPED A HAIRLESS DOG BREED CALLED

XOLOITZCUINTLI.

THE DOGS WERE THOUGHT TO PROTECT HOMES FROM EVIL SPIRITS.

Are you a fan of FANG from the *HARRY POTTER* films?

In real life, fully grown NEAPOLITAN MASTIFFS can weigh over

68 KILOGRAMS
(150 POUNDS)!

It is a MYTH that dogs feel GUILT.

THEY ARE PROBABLY FEELING **FEAR** INSTEAD.

DOG WEE CAN CORRODE METAL.

GLOSSARY

anxiety feeling of worry or fear

ban forbid something

combat fighting between people or armies

corrode wear away gradually due to a chemical reaction

descendant person or animal who can trace their family roots back to one individual

domesticated bred to live or work with people

honorary degree degree given by a university without the person (or animal) doing the usual work for a degree, such as sitting exams. It is given as a sign of honour or respect for the individual.

influential having influence over people

instinct behaviour that is natural, rather than learned

livestock animals kept for use, especially farm animals

membrane thin layer of tissue forming a barrier or lining

oxytocin hormone that makes humans and animals feel happy

receptor cell in the body that sends signals to the sensory nerves

seizure sudden attack of illness

vital required for sustaining life

BOOKS

Designer Dog Projects (Pet Projects), Isabel Thomas (Raintree, 2016)

Dogs (Animal Abilities), Charlotte Guillain (Raintree, 2014)

Dogs (Animal Family Albums), Paul Mason (Raintree, 2014)

The Truth About Dogs: What Dogs Do When You're Not Looking (Pets Undercover), Mary Colson (Raintree, 2018)

WEBSITES

Find out more about dogs.
www.dkfindout.com/uk/animals-and-nature/dogs

Learn more about your favourite animals.
https://young.rspca.org.uk/kids/animals

INDEX

Raintree is an imprint of Capstone Global Library Limited, a company incorporated in England and Wales having its registered office at 264 Banbury Road, Oxford, OX2 7DY – Registered company number: 6695582

www.raintree.co.uk
myorders@raintree.co.uk

Original illustrations © Capstone Global Library Ltd
Originated by Capstone Global Library Ltd
Printed and bound in India

ISBN 978 1 4747 6563 3
22 21 20 19 18
10 9 8 7 6 5 4 3 2 1

British Library Cataloguing in Publication Data
A full catalogue record for this book is available from the British Library.

Acknowledgements
We would like to thank the following for permission to reproduce photographs: Shutterstock: Victoria Rak, cover (top left), Dorottya Mathe, cover (top right), Dorottya Mathe, cover (bottom left), Kalamurzing, cover (bottom right), Dmitry Pichugin, 2, Jim Cumming, 3, Dora Zett, 4, Javier Brosch, 5, Javier Brosch, 6, vichie81, 7, Eric Isselee, 9-10, Rickshu, 11, Patryk Kosmider, 12, Weerameth Weerachotewong, 13, Sarah Lew, 15, Dorottya Mathe, 18, M.Stasy, 18, Eric Isselee, 19, DenisNata, 20 (police dog), Talaj, 20, (police hat), Luka Djuricic, 22, otsphoto, 24 (dog side view) wavebreakmedia, 24 (girl side view), Digital Deliverance, 25, Zivica Kerkez, 26, Sonsedska Yuliia, 27, Eric Isselee, 27 (sad dog), Ermolaev Alexander, 28, Africa Studio, 29, Shevs, 30, kittipong053, 32, Dorottya Mathe, 33, Yuliya Evstratenko, 34, Javier Brosch, 35, Eric Isselee, 36, M. Unal Ozmen, 38 (popcorn), Jiri Hera, 38 (chips), Napat, 38 (paw), Ivanova N, 40, art nick, 41, Alexonline, 42, Lindsay Helms, 43, Vector_dream_team, 44, wolfness72, 45, Lena Ivanova, 46, eurobanks, 47 (dog hug), iko, 47 (doctor dog), ign, 48, Olga Kashubin, 50, Durd Yu, 51 (dog), Laborant, 51 (cake), Yezepchyk Oleksandr, 53 (Egyptian tomb), ARTSILENSE, 53 (dog), RickDeacon, 54 (alps), Nadezhda V. Kulagina, 54 (dog), Azuzl, 56, Blackspring, 57, Eric Isselee, 59, Illustratiostock, 61, Eric Isselee, 62 (dog), Mega Pixel, 62 (snorkel), rzoze19, 63, Dora Zett, 65, Eric Isselee, 67, MarkVanDykePhotography, 69, Jet Cat Studio, 70, Eric Isselee, 72, Annette Shaff, 73-74, Ljupco Smokovski, 76, Javier Brosch, 78, Dean Drobot, 79, Nikolai Tsvetkov, 81 (ewok dog), Ryan Tanguilan, 81 (forest), Nenilkime, 82, Ermolaev Alexander, 83 (little dog), Eric Isselee, 83 (big dog), Eric Isselee, 84 (chihuahua), Csanad Kiss, 84 (dachshund), cvalle, 85 (dog), chrisbrignell, 85 (security hat), oksana2010, 88, Eric Isselee, 89, Javier Brosch, 90, SikorskiFotografie, 92, Djomas, 93, Fotoeventis, 95, Ruth Black, 96, LightField Studios, 97, schubbel, 98, Everett - Art, 100 (George Washington), golfyinterlude, 100 (beagle), Eric Isselee, 100 (dalmation), Kuznetsov Alexey, 103, Erik Lam, 105, Susan Schmitz, 106, Shevs, 107, iStock/Getty Images Plus: SolStock, 64, Preto_perola, 100 (frame)

Design Elements by Shutterstock, Getty Images and DynamoLimited

TH 7/5/19